UNREASONABLE SEARCH AND SEIZURE

DEAN GALIANO

rosen publishing's
rosen central

New York

Published in 2011 by The Rosen Publishing Group, Inc.
29 East 21st Street, New York, NY 10010

Copyright © 2011 by The Rosen Publishing Group, Inc.

First Edition

Library of Congress Cataloging-in-Publication Data

Galiano, Dean.
The Fourth Amendment : unreasonable search and seizure/Dean Galiano.
    p. cm. — (Amendments to the United States Constitution : the Bill of Rights)
Includes bibliographical references and index.
ISBN 978-1-4488-1259-2 (library binding)
ISBN 978-1-4488-2305-5 (pbk.)
ISBN 978-1-4488-2315-4 (6-pack)
1. Searches and seizures—United States—Juvenile literature. 2. United States. Constitution.
4th Amendment—Juvenile literature. I. Title.
KF9630.G35 2011
345.73'0522—dc22

                                                                                    2010017394

Manufactured in the United States of America

CPSIA Compliance Information: Batch #W11YA: For further information, contact Rosen Publishing, New York, New York, at 1-800-237-9932.

On the cover: Left: A Transportation Security Administration (TSA) cargo inspector guides her dog to inspect cargo during a security demonstration. Center: An airport police officer searches an abandoned bag at Los Angeles International Airport. Right: An officer in the Los Angeles Police Department's gang unit searches a man. This sort of search by police is permitted by the Fourth Amendment.

CONTENTS

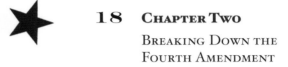

INTRODUCTION

I n 2001, the Supreme Court of the United States heard the seminal Fourth Amendment case *Kyllo v. United States*. At stake was the protection of individuals' Fourth Amendment rights versus the need for law enforcement to prosecute criminal behavior. The Court would have to choose a side and rule accordingly.

The *Kyllo* case revolved around the use of a new technology called thermal imaging. In 1992, Special Agent William Elliot used a thermal-imaging device to detect the level of heat within Danny Kyllo's home. Elliot suspected that Kyllo was growing marijuana in his home. Elliot knew that special lights were needed to grow marijuana indoors, and

Danny Kyllo is pictured here in front of his home in 2001, days before the U.S. Supreme Court prepared to hear oral arguments in his now famous case.

that these lights generated a great deal of heat. The thermal-imaging device showed that an unusually large amount of heat was being generated in Kyllo's house. With the help of this discovery, Elliot was able to secure a warrant from a judge to search Kyllo's home.

Upon conducting the search, law enforcement officers found a grow farm consisting of more than one hundred marijuana plants in Kyllo's home. Based upon this evidence, a grand jury indicted Kyllo for the crime of manufacturing marijuana.

After his indictment, Kyllo moved to suppress the evidence gathered at his home. One of his arguments for the suppression of the evidence was that the use of a thermal imager was an unreasonable Fourth Amendment search. The Fourth Amendment states:

> The right of the people to be secure in their persons, houses, papers, and effects, against unreasonable searches and seizures, shall not be violated, and no Warrants shall issue, but upon probable cause, supported by Oath or affirmation, and particularly describing the place to be searched, and the persons or things to be seized.

Kyllo argued that a warrant was required for the thermal imager to be used in the first place. The trial court denied Kyllo's motion, and he was subsequently convicted. Kyllo appealed, or petitioned against, the decision. A court of appeals heard the case three times before coming to the conclusion that the use of thermal imaging in this case was not a violation of Kyllo's Fourth Amendment rights. Kyllo, unsatisfied with the ruling, made one final appeal to the Supreme Court.

In a 5–4 decision, the Supreme Court reversed the lower courts' previous rulings and declared that the targeting of a home by law officers with a thermal imager is in fact a search under the Fourth Amendment. The Court stated, "At the very core of the Fourth Amendment stands the right of a man to retreat into his own home and there be free from unreasonable governmental intrusion."

The Supreme Court's ruling in the *Kyllo* case asserted the rights of the individual over the powers of the government. Kyllo was illegally growing marijuana in his home, but this did not give the U.S. government permission to ignore his Fourth Amendment rights. It was Elliot's legal obligation to obtain a warrant before searching Kyllo's home. The request to a judge for a search warrant is a way of checking the power of law enforcement officials, and such checks are necessary to ensure that law enforcement does not abuse its power.

The *Kyllo* decision was also important because it addressed technology as it relates to the Fourth Amendment. The Court asserted that unless a warrant had been granted beforehand, the use of any new technology to survey private property was likely a violation of the Fourth Amendment.

The Founding Fathers could not have possibly imagined the technical innovations that have been developed since the Bill of Rights was written. It is up to the Supreme Court to ensure that the spirit of the amendment remains intact as unprecedented situations arise.

CHAPTER ONE

THE LONG ROAD TO BASIC HUMAN RIGHTS

L ife in eighteenth-century colonial America was difficult. Harsh winters, disease, and hostile Native Americans were just a few of the challenges that the colonists were forced to contend with on a daily basis. Through all of these hardships, however, the colonists were fortified by the knowledge that they were given opportunities in the colonies that they would not have had back in England.

England was a country with a rigid class system. The class that a person was born into largely determined his or her station in life. A person who was born poor in England had very few, if any, opportunities to better him- or herself. The colonists, although frequently challenged by life in America, still had the means to better their places in the world.

This print depicts the landing of the Pilgrims at Plymouth Rock in 1620. Like many colonists, they braved severe conditions for the chance at a better life for themselves and their families.

In America, they could, through hard work and diligence, become landowners and businessmen—opportunities that had been out of their reach back in Europe.

The Seeds of Revolt

In the early days of the colonies, relations between the colonists and the British were generally amicable, or friendly. The relationship began to deteriorate in 1763, however, shortly after the French and Indian War. The expense of the war left the British with a great deal of debt. In order to pay this debt, the British raised taxes throughout the empire.

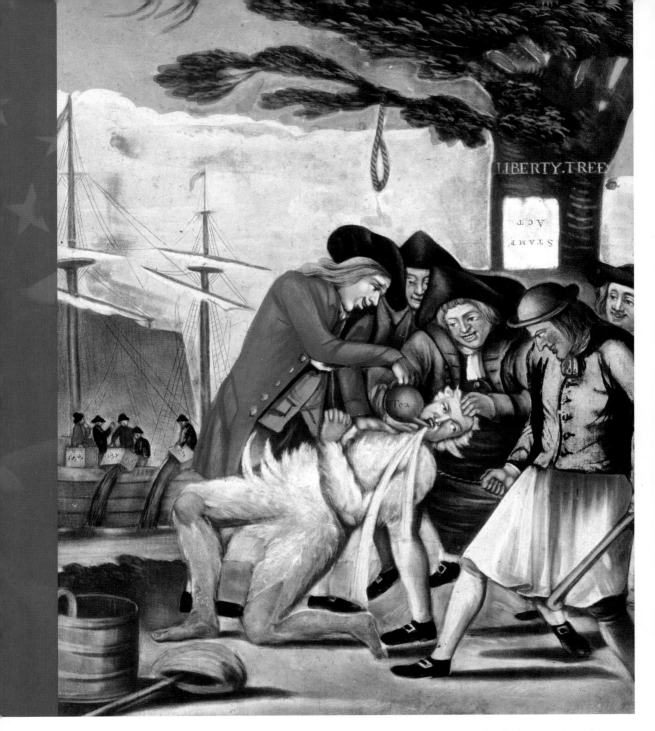

This political cartoon, captioned "The Bostonians Paying the Excise Man," shows a British customs official being abused by angry colonists shortly before the American Revolution.

Taxes such as those under the Sugar Act were placed on goods imported into the colonies, and undue financial burdens were placed on the colonists.

Of all the new taxes, it was the Stamp Act of 1765 that most angered the colonists. This act imposed a tax on all printed documents. The colonists were forced to purchase official stamps before they could issue any written works, such as newspapers, books, legal documents, and even marriage licenses.

The colonists' anger over the taxes was further stoked by the fact that these duties were paid to a government in which they were not represented. This meant that the colonists had no voice in matters of state. They had no legal way to argue or influence the laws passed across the Atlantic Ocean. Whatever laws Parliament passed, the colonists were forced to live with.

The Writs of Assistance

To the colonists, British enforcement of the Stamp Act was as much a source of irritation as the tax itself was. Parliament issued writs of assistance to British customs inspectors in order to enforce the collection of taxes. These writs gave inspectors the right to forcibly search the home or workplace of any colonist in order to find evidence of tax evasion.

One particularly irksome aspect of these searches was that the inspectors were not required to show any evidence of tax evasion in order to conduct their searches. They could simply enter a property and ransack the place in an attempt to find papers that did not have the necessary stamps. It was these types of searches that eventually led the Founding Fathers to include the Fourth Amendment in the Bill of Rights when they were forming their new government.

Search and Seizure in British Law

The Fourth Amendment grew directly out of the mistreatment of colonists by the British with their use of the writs of assistance. The call against general warrants was not unique to the colonists, however. British citizens themselves had long protested the use of general warrants. The closely held belief that "Every man's house is his castle" was an idea much celebrated by the English. This idea was demonstrated in *Semayne's Case*, which was decided in 1603.

Semayne's Case was instrumental in recognizing the right of a homeowner to defend his or her house against unlawful entry, even by agents of the king himself. While *Semayne's Case* was important in its defense of individual rights against governmental search and seizure, it was not in any way a complete victory. It still recognized that the crown could continue intrusions into citizens' homes when matters of "public welfare" were at stake.

Building a Better Government

The British continued to vex the colonies with their unjust practice of taxation without representation. The Townshend Acts (1767) and the Tea Act (1773) further angered the colonists. By the time of the First Continental Congress in 1774, the colonists were all too familiar with the abuses that an unchecked government imposes upon its subjects. They realized that any powers given to government in order to maintain a society must be balanced by specific rights and freedoms granted to the people. They determined that a proper and just government must be managed and controlled by a system of checks and balances. They used this concept as a framework for the U.S. Constitution.

The Continental Congress appointed George Washington as commander in chief of the Continental Army on June 19, 1775, because of his previous military experience and in the hope that a leader from Virginia could unite the colonies.

Delegates from each colony attended the First Continental Congress. One of the principal achievements of the Congress was the drafting and ratification of a declaration of personal rights. This declaration was a forerunner to the Bill of Rights. It guaranteed the colonialists the rights to life, liberty, property, assembly, and trial by jury.

The delegates also put together several lists of grievances. These denounced England's policy of taxation without representation as well as the presence of the British army in the colonies without the consent of the colonialists. In 1775, the colonists sent their grievances to the king of England, hoping for the best but also well prepared for the worst.

King George III was in no mood to negotiate with the colonists. The British military was large and powerful. The king would use it to enforce British law in the colonies whether the colonialists liked it or not. In April 1775, the first shots of the American Revolution were fired in Lexington, Massachusetts.

The Articles of Confederation

The American War of Independence concluded in 1783. At that time the thirteen colonies were united under an agreement called the Articles of Confederation. The articles were America's first attempt to govern itself as an independent nation.

The Articles of Confederation provided the first basic framework for the government of the newly created United States. They fell short, however, in establishing a strong central government. Without a strong central government, there was no way to bond the states together in a practical manner.

When the articles were drawn up, the colonists were extremely wary of any sort of powerful central government. The document gave most governmental power to the states of the confederation and very little to a central government. The states could only act together in dealing with matters of extreme national importance, such as war.

The articles had several problems. One issue was that unanimous approval was required from all states in order for any changes to be made to the articles. Such approval was nearly impossible to achieve. Another problem was that the articles gave the weak central government no power to tax the individual states in order to maintain a national treasury. This made it nearly impossible for the central government to fund a national army. The effective regulation of commerce between states was also an issue.

In 1787, Alexander Hamilton realized that the Articles of Confederation were inadequate in holding the United States together in any functional way. He suggested that delegates from each state meet in Philadelphia to create a more comprehensive government.

From Confederation to Nation

In 1788, the Constitution of the United States was written and ratified. The Constitution is a brilliant and far-reaching document that delineates the powers of the federal and the state governments with a system of checks and balances.

The Constitution is comprehensive in outlining the powers of the federal and state governments. However, shortly after its final draft was completed, George Mason, a delegate from the state of Virginia noted that it said nothing in regards to the rights of the people. Mason was very bothered by this omission. After all, it had been only twelve years earlier that the British government had been stomping all over the personal freedoms of the colonists. Now, a new powerful government was being created. What guarantee did its citizens have that this government would not trample their rights as well?

Mason was not the only delegate who was alarmed by the omission of individual liberties from the Constitution. James Madison and Thomas Jefferson were equally concerned. Jefferson wanted to see provisions in the Constitution that guaranteed people freedom of religion, freedom of the press, and protection against standing armies.

By June 1788, nine states had ratified the Constitution. Technically only nine states needed to ratify it for it to become the law of the land. However, the fact that Virginia and New York had not ratified the document caused a great deal of concern. Virginia and New York were large

James Madison is known today as the father of the Constitution. Madison wrote the Bill of Rights in 1791. He later served as the fourth president of the United States.

and powerful states, and without the support of these two states, many delegates felt that the Constitution could not ultimately hold the new nation together. In addition, five of the nine states that had ratified the Constitution did so on the condition that amendments ensuring human rights would be added immediately.

In September 1791, when the first Congress met in New York City, calls for amendments protecting individual rights were nearly unanimous. A few months earlier, at the urging of several states, James Madison had drawn up twelve amendments that he felt addressed the concerns of the delegates. These amendments were presented to Congress, and by December 1791, the ten amendments we know as the Bill of Rights were ratified.

CHAPTER TWO

BREAKING DOWN THE FOURTH AMENDMENT

The Fourth Amendment was born out of the experience of the colonists suffering at the hands of British law. The colonists had resented general warrants, specifically the writs of assistance that allowed British officials to enter their homes at will to search for evidence of tax evasion. With these memories still fresh in their minds, it is no wonder that the carefully crafted wording of the Fourth Amendment found its way into the Bill of Rights of the U.S. Constitution.

The notion that a government should be limited in its power to intrude into a citizen's home was certainly a priority for the Founding Fathers when they crafted their new system of government. The idea itself, however, was not a new one. This premise had long been argued by British legal theorists, who themselves were bothered by the intrusive nature of the general search warrant. Such warrants had enjoyed a long history in England, predating the American colonies.

General Warrants

The writs of assistance are an example of a general warrant. A general warrant is one that is not specific in who it is issued to, what place is to be searched, or what is to be searched for. Before the writs of assistance were created by Parliament to enforce tax collection in the colonies, British law had long used such general warrants to collect taxes in England.

From about 1290, Parliament gave royal officials nearly unlimited power to search persons, houses, and ships. These searches were done in an effort to collect customs taxes on products imported to and exported from Britain. In 1662, Parliament formalized the method for customs searches, and out of this formalization the writs of assistance were born. The writs gave customs officials the power to demand assistance from other officers, as well as bystanders, in their searches.

In 1763, a government search and seizure case in Britain, involving a member of Parliament named John Wilkes, came to the attention of the American colonists. The case involved governmental search and seizure of the property of private citizens using a general warrant. British crown officers had searched Wilkes's home and discovered papers that expressed critical opinions of the king. Upon finding the papers, they were confiscated and Wilkes was arrested.

Wilkes, fighting for his rights, sued every official that was involved with the warrant. In a trial on July 6, 1763, the chief justice of the Court of Common Pleas criticized the general nature of the warrant. The

This portrait of John Wilkes was painted in 1768. Wilkes's legal victory over the British practice of general warrants made him a hero to the colonists.

warrant had specified no particular person and had been issued without a formal complaint under oath, thus the warrant had been issued without probable cause. When the case came before the full court, Chief Justice Charles Pratt ruled that the warrant's authority for general search and general arrest violated English common law.

Wilkes's successful defense against general warrants made him a hero to colonial Americans. American newspapers printed Wilkes's speeches as well as summaries of the trial. Wilkes's victory against British imperial tyranny was still fresh in the minds of the Founding Fathers when they called the Continental Congress to meet in 1774. At this gathering, they roundly condemned any and all general searches. By 1791, any such searches by the federal government were made illegal in the United States thanks to the wording of the Fourth Amendment.

The Fourth Amendment in Action

The Fourth Amendment protects people from "unreasonable" searches of their persons, houses, papers, and effects. This raises the question: What is a reasonable search? The text of the amendment itself does not offer a definition of either a "reasonable" or "unreasonable" search. For the most part judges and the Supreme Court have looked to the next part of the amendment in helping them to determine what constitutes a reasonable search.

The Fourth Amendment specifies that "no Warrants shall be issued, but upon probable cause . . . and supported by Oath or affirmation . . ." Built into the language of the amendment, then, is the requirement that a warrant be issued before a search is carried out. Without a warrant, a federal governmental search of an individual's house, person, papers, and effects is deemed to be unconstitutional.

It is essential that a search warrant be issued by a neutral magistrate, such as a judge. The presence of a neutral magistrate protects constitutional rights and limits the power of law enforcement.

The need for a warrant to be obtained before an officer of the law can conduct a search is a crucial element of the Fourth Amendment. This requirement is based upon the principle that law enforcement officers need to have their powers checked in some way. Although the text does not specify this, it is commonly understood that the person who issues a search warrant must be a neutral magistrate. This means that the person who issues a warrant must be someone who has no vested interest in prosecuting the person named in the warrant. Since a judge is not part of the police force and is charged with being impartial, the neutral magistrate is, in most cases, a judge.

Amendment in Action: *Coolidge v. New Hampshire*

The Supreme Court case *Coolidge v. New Hampshire* (1971) offers a good example of why a neutral magistrate is so important in the process of obtaining a search warrant. In this case, the attorney general of New Hampshire—who was also the chief prosecutor of the case—issued the search warrant for a murder investigation. The Court settled this obvious conflict of interest when they threw out all of the evidence gathered under the warrant.

In ruling on the case, Justice Potter Stewart held the opinion that the warrant authorizing the seizure of Coolidge's automobile was invalid based upon the fact that it was not issued by a "neutral and detached magistrate."

Supreme Court Justice Potter Stewart felt that a neutral magistrate was essential to the process of obtaining a legal search warrant.

In order for a law officer to justify a request for a search warrant, that official must convince a neutral magistrate that there is probable cause for the warrant to be issued. Evidence for probable cause must be supported by facts. This means that an official cannot get a warrant based upon mere suspicion. An officer can suspect that somebody is involved in a crime and that there is evidence to be found at that person's home, but without any facts to justify such a suspicion, a search warrant should not be issued by a judge.

In addition to presenting probable cause to a neutral magistrate, an official must also swear that the evidence he or she is providing to obtain the warrant is factual. Any warrant that is obtained by lying to a judge or magistrate is unconstitutional. If it is observed that an official has lied in order to get a search warrant, any evidence recovered from that search is not allowable in court, even if such evidence would have otherwise led to a conviction.

Once probable cause has been presented and affirmed, an official must also describe to a magistrate what crime has been committed and where specifically the search will be conducted. This wording is very specific in the Fourth Amendment for good reason. The Founding Fathers detested the idea of any sort of general warrants, such as the writs of assistance. It was important to them that warrants be of a specific nature in order to protect the rights of the individual.

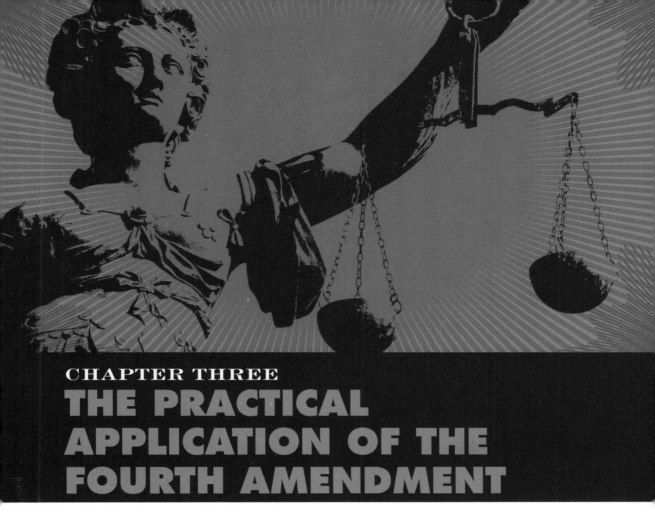

CHAPTER THREE

THE PRACTICAL APPLICATION OF THE FOURTH AMENDMENT

Threne first major Supreme Court decision involving the Fourth Amendment came in the 1886 case *Boyd v. United States*. This case centered around E. A. Boyd, whose company had been contracted by the government to supply glass for several federal buildings in Philadelphia. Boyd offered to discount his finished glass to the government on the condition that the government would not make him pay duties on the raw glass that he imported for the job. Over time, the government began to suspect that Boyd was actually importing more duty-free glass than was needed for the government contract, thus getting duty-free glass to use for other jobs, which was illegal.

The government took Boyd to court, demanding that he give up the lucrative contract. Once in court, the trial judge demanded that Boyd present each and every invoice for the glass he had imported. At first Boyd resisted the judge's order, but eventually he gave in and handed over all of his invoices. Based upon this evidence he was convicted.

Boyd was unhappy that he had been forced to hand over his invoices in court. He went on to appeal the decision to the Supreme Court. He appealed on the basis of his Fourth Amendment right of freedom from unreasonable searches and seizures and his Fifth Amendment right against self-incrimination.

The Supreme Court carefully considered whether Boyd's Fourth and Fifth amendment rights had been violated. They determined that by ordering Boyd to produce his invoices, the trial judge had indeed violated his rights under both amendments. They ruled that the right to be "secure" in one's person or dwelling means that a person should never be required to give up evidence that might be self-incriminating. The Court went on to order that a new trial take place, this time without the inclusion of Boyd's unconstitutionally acquired invoices as evidence.

The Exclusionary Rule

While the Supreme Court's decision to hold a new trial in the *Boyd* case worked, it was not practical for the court system to have trials repeated. The expense and time would be too great to retry many cases in this manner. Based upon this, the Supreme Court created the exclusionary rule to deal with evidence that had been acquired in violation of the Fourth Amendment.

The Supreme Court first used the exclusionary rule in the 1914 case *Weeks v. United States*. The *Weeks* case involved the arrest of Fremont

Weeks and the warrantless search of his home. Weeks was convicted based upon the ill-gotten evidence. He went on to appeal the conviction to the Supreme Court based upon his Fourth Amendment rights.

The Court overturned Weeks's conviction. In the process it adopted the new policy that any evidence that was seized in violation of the Fourth Amendment was to be excluded from trial.

Bringing the Fourth Amendment to the People

Prior to 1961, only federal cases had to conform to the Fourth Amendment. For nearly two centuries after the ratification of the Fourth Amendment, American citizens could be denied their federal Fourth Amendment rights in any local or state court. In essence this situation rendered the Fourth Amendment little more than a symbol of the Founding Fathers' good intentions.

The Supreme Court had made it clear in its decision in the 1833 case *Barron v. Baltimore* that the Bill of Rights did not apply to actions taken by local or state governments. This decision stood with very little thought given to it until after the Civil War when the Fourteenth Amendment was ratified.

The Fourteenth Amendment did a number of things. In relation to the Bill of Rights, it extended the protections of federal law to all citizens in all states. Since all U.S. citizens were entitled to the protections of the Bill of Rights in federal matters, the Fourteenth Amendment should have thus extended those protections to state actions. These protections were painfully slow in arriving, however, as conservative Supreme Court justices limited the extension of the guarantees provided by the Bill of Rights.

Mapp v. Ohio

In 1961, the Supreme Court finally ruled that the Bill of Rights did indeed apply to the states. By doing so, the Court put an end to the great paradox of the Bill of Rights, which guaranteed the rights of individuals on the federal level but not on the state level. This history-making ruling was made in the *Mapp v. Ohio* case.

In 1957, the police came to the home of Dollree Mapp demanding that she allow them to search her home. They were looking for a person who was wanted for questioning in a recent bombing. Mapp did not let the police in, but rather demanded that they first provide a warrant before searching her home. The officers, not possessing a warrant at the time, left.

The police officers came back shortly and forced their way into Mapp's home. They waved a piece of paper quickly in the air as they entered, which they claimed was a warrant. Officers went on to search her house, and though they did not find the person they were looking for in connection with the bombing, they did find books and photographs that were considered obscene under Ohio law. Based

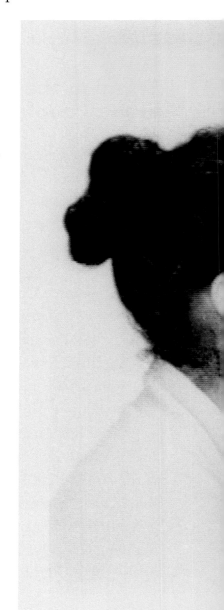

Dollree Mapp's conviction under Ohio state law was later overruled by the Supreme Court with the application of the exclusionary rule.

upon this evidence, Mapp was arrested and convicted of possession of obscene materials.

In 1961, Mapp's appeal eventually reached the Supreme Court. In a landmark decision, the Court overruled Mapp's conviction by applying

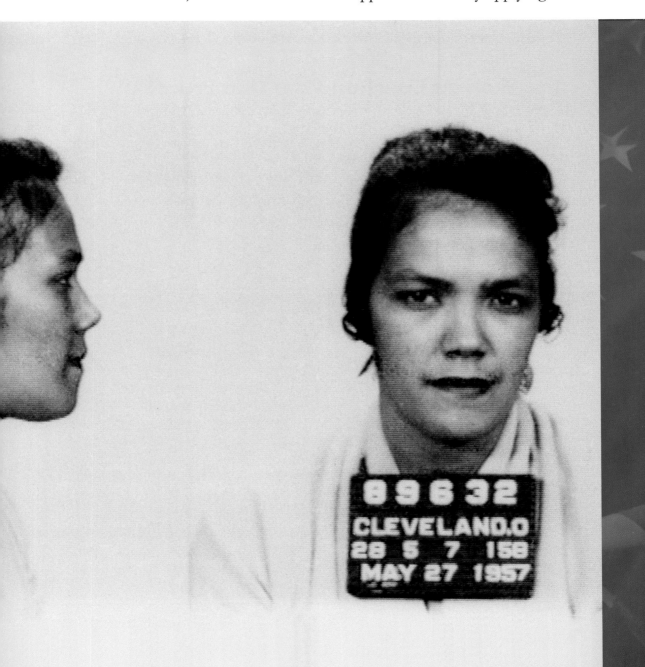

the exclusionary rule to the evidence that the police had collected to convict her. By applying the exclusionary rule, the Court rendered the evidence inadmissible during trial. The importance of the *Mapp* case cannot be underestimated because the Supreme Court, for the first time, had applied the exclusionary rule to the states, thus finally ensuring Fourth Amendment rights for citizens at the state level.

The Warren Court and the Due Process Revolution

When Earl Warren accepted the position of chief justice of the Supreme Court in 1953, he faced the challenge of dealing with a deeply divided Court. Some of the justices felt strongly that the Court should have a more active role in the application of justice, while other justices favored the path of judicial restraint.

Controversial Aspects of the Exclusionary Rule

The decision of the Supreme Court in the *Mapp* case, which forced states to follow the exclusionary rule, was not without controversy. Some people felt that this rule helped criminals to go free. They argued that evidence that was not allowed in court because of a technical search issue was still evidence of a crime that had been committed.

Others, including the majority of the Warren Court, felt that it was more important to uphold the highest principles of American liberty than to prosecute the criminal. Protecting these principles meant following as closely as possible due process of law as outlined in the Constitution. The majority of the Warren Court argued that if following due process meant that sometimes the guilty went free, then so be it, as it was more important to them that the innocent were protected under the law.

Warren proved himself to be very effective in building consensus among the justices. The history-making case *Brown v. Board of Education* (1954) was one of the first that Warren had to deal with as chief justice. In this case, the Court overturned the long controversial "separate but equal" doctrine, thus opening the path for the racial integration of America's public schools.

The Warren Court staunchly defended the individual rights of Americans. Warren considered it the job of the Court to prohibit the government from acting unfairly against the individual. Between 1961

Chief Justice Earl Warren (*pictured front center*) presided over a Supreme Court that handed down rulings in pivotal cases such as *Mapp v. Ohio* (1961) and *Miranda v. Arizona* (1966). The Warren Court was a champion of individual liberties.

and 1969, the Warren Court accomplished what previous Courts had resisted: it applied the procedural guarantees of the Bill of Rights to the states' administration of criminal justice.

In the rulings of cases such as *Mapp v. Ohio* (1961), which extended the exclusionary rule to the states, and *Miranda v. Arizona* (1966),

Searches in Schools

There have been a few important Supreme Court cases that have revolved around the Fourth Amendment protections that students should enjoy at schools. In one important case, *New Jersey v. T.L.O.* (1984), the Court ruled that the Fourth Amendment did indeed apply to the public school system. The Court went on to explain, however, that in the search process, school officials should not be held to the same standards as law enforcement. Instead, school officials should be held to a more general standard of whether a search is "reasonable under the circumstances." This means that the search must be performed only if the official expects to turn up evidence that a student has violated school rules. The Court also requires that the search not be unnecessarily intrusive.

In the 1995 decision of *Vernonia School District v. Acton*, the Court stated that, while a child has an expectation of privacy, this expectation is less than what an adult enjoys. This language grants school officials leeway in deciding what types of searches are "reasonable" when it comes to students.

A K-9 narcotics detection officer and his dog search lockers for illegal drugs in an Arizona high school.

which ensured that the police read a suspect his or her rights before any questioning could occur, Warren established the Court as the ultimate protector of civil rights and civil liberties.

Rolling Back Individual Rights for the Greater Good

The Supreme Court of the 1970s and 1980s, led by Chief Justice Warren Earl Burger, tended to interpret the Bill of Rights in a different manner than did the Warren Court. Crime was on the rise in America in the 1970s. The Supreme Court felt strongly that it needed to protect the safety of the general public, even if it meant interpreting the Bill of Rights in a way that put a higher priority on the safety of the public than on the rights of the individual.

In taking a tougher stance on crime, the Burger Court tended to be more tolerant of police behavior. This was apparent in a number of Fourth Amendment decisions that the Burger Court handed down.

One notable change was the Burger Court's lowering of the requirements for what they felt constituted a valid police search. In the 1971 *United States v. Harris* ruling, the Court ruled that a suspect's reputation alone was sufficient to seek a search warrant. This decision significantly altered the concept of proving "probable cause" to a judge in the acquisition of a search warrant. A warrant could now be issued based on rumor or an anonymous informant's tip to the police.

The Burger Court also made a number of exceptions to the exclusionary rule that the Warren Court had previously imposed upon the states. In 1984, the Court made two important exceptions to the rule. The decisions in these cases marked a pullback of Fourth Amendment rights from the accused.

In the *United States v. Leon* case, a warrant had been issued by a judicial officer to search the homes and cars of various people suspected of drug-related criminal activity. The suspects were convicted based upon the evidence discovered. The warrant, however, was issued based on dated, five-month-old information from an informant whose reliability was questionable. A federal court of appeals subsequently overturned the conviction, based upon the premise that the information used to obtain the warrant did not support probable cause. The controversial case eventually found its way to the Supreme Court.

The Court overruled the decision of the appeals court and declared that the search was indeed valid. They believed that the police were acting in "good faith" and that therefore the search should be considered legal. By "good faith" the Court meant that the police had followed

Chief Justice Warren Earl Burger (*pictured front center*) felt that protecting the safety of the general public was as important as protecting individual rights.

procedure and had taken time to present their case to get a warrant. The Court held that the police had no reason to believe that the warrant was issued in an improper manner. The Court ruled that as long as the police were acting in good faith, the evidence should be admissible, even if the warrant itself was not valid.

The other key exception that the Court granted in 1984 to the exclusionary rule was termed "inevitable discovery." Inevitable discovery means that, as long as the prosecution can demonstrate that legally gathered evidence would have eventually led to the discovery of any illegally seized evidence, the illegally seized evidence can still be used in court.

The Rehnquist Court

By 1980, the crime rate in the Unites States remained uncomfortably high. A 1982 report issued by the Attorney General's Task Force on Violent Crime stated that the costs to society of the exclusionary rule were unacceptably high. The federal government had declared war on crime. Numerous attempts were made during President Ronald Reagan's first administration to further restrict or abandon the exclusionary rule altogether. It was in this environment that William Rehnquist was appointed chief justice.

Rehnquist had always been dissatisfied with the Warren Court's ruling in *Mapp v. Ohio*, and he vehemently opposed the exclusionary rule. He felt that excluding relevant evidence from an illegal search hampered the police in their ability to administer justice. He was less concerned that the police might conduct illegal searches than he was that criminals might be allowed to get away with illegal activities.

The Rehnquist Court first addressed the exclusionary rule in the 1987 case *Illinois v. Krull*. In this case police had relied upon a state law, which was later declared unconstitutional, to authorize a search. The

Chief Justice William Rehnquist was nominated by President Ronald Reagan on June 17, 1986. Rehnquist strongly opposed the exclusionary rule, as he felt that it hampered law enforcement's ability to convict dangerous criminals.

Court decided to extend the good faith rule in this case and allowed the evidence to stand. In a later case, *Arizona v. Evans* (1995), the Rehnquist Court extended the good faith rule yet again. In this case, the Court found that even though a warrant was issued in error, based upon a mistake in an official database, the evidence should still be admissible.

Searches Allowable Without a Warrant

In some cases, the Court has acknowledged that there are situations where searches may be performed without first getting a warrant, in order to protect the public. Determining which exact type of search is "reasonable" however, has not been without controversy.

Consensual Searches

The first, and most simple, category of search where no warrant is needed is when the search is consensual. If an officer asks permission to search a suspect's home and the suspect gives permission to do so, the search is considered constitutional and any and all evidence discovered in the search is allowable in court. The suspect, by allowing the search, has essentially waived his or her Fourth Amendment rights.

Searches Performed by Private Citizens

The Fourth Amendment does not cover searches performed by a private citizen. The Fourth Amendment covers only governmental searches. A person's employer, for example, may search his or her desk or other work areas without violating the Fourth Amendment in any way whatsoever.

"Plain View" Searches

The "plain view" exception to the warrant requirement allows police to seize any evidence not specifically covered by a warrant as long as they are lawfully in the area to begin with and the evidence is in plain view. So, if the police have a warrant to search for a gun used in a robbery, and they see the actual stolen goods lying around, they can seize these goods even though they are not mentioned in the warrant.

Another type of plain view search is if the police actually witness an illegal activity. For example, police witness a man doing illegal drugs in public. Upon witnessing the illegal act they can search the man and confiscate any drugs that he has on him.

Frisking

Frisking refers to the practice of a police officer "patting down" a person who is suspected of having committed or is on his or her way to

committing a crime. In the 1968 *Terry v. Ohio* case, the Court found that police must have some capacity to search a suspect for weapons. If a weapon could be felt in the process of patting down a suspect, then the police could reach into the suspect's clothing and confiscate the weapon.

In 1993, the Court expanded this type of search to include the confiscation any sort of illegal items, such as drugs.

Arrests

During an arrest, the police have the right to search a person and the area around him or her without a warrant. There are three main reasons for this, all of which the Supreme Court has decided are in the public interest:

- The suspect might be concealing weapons.
- To prevent the escape of the suspect.
- To prevent the destruction of any evidence at a crime scene.

Police are allowed to frisk suspects without a warrant to determine if they are carrying weapons.

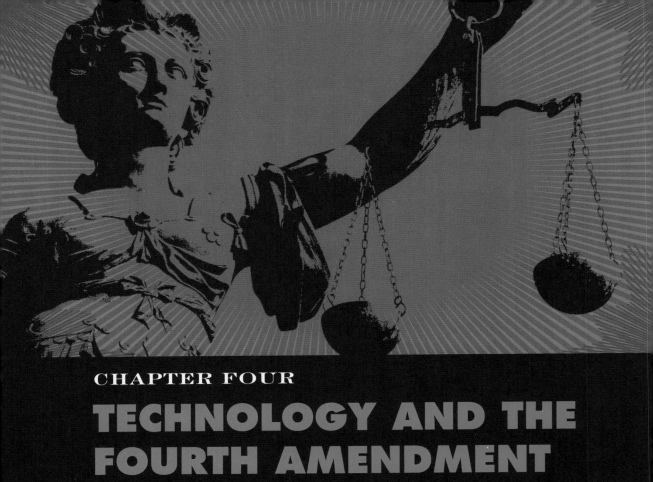

CHAPTER FOUR

TECHNOLOGY AND THE FOURTH AMENDMENT

W hen the Fourth Amendment was ratified in 1791, there was no way that the Founding Fathers could imagine all of the new technology that the government could someday put to use in collecting information in criminal investigations. There have been a number of Supreme Court cases in which technology has played a pivotal role.

Vehicles

The first mass-produced automobiles began rolling off assembly lines in America in the early 1900s. Since then, vehicles have historically

Arizona Highway Patrol officers search a van for drugs near Tucson. In most law enforcement situations, the Court allows searches of vehicles without a warrant as long as probable cause exists.

presented challenges to interpreting the Fourth Amendment. While not a person's home, a car certainly does seem to qualify in some way as part of a person's effects. For nearly a century, the Supreme Court has had to weigh carefully the protections that automobiles should enjoy under the Fourth Amendment.

Over the years, the Court has for the most part ruled that vehicles can be searched without a warrant as long as probable cause exists to search the vehicle in question. The Court bases this stance on the fact that, unlike a house, a car or truck can be moved, so there is a very real danger of evidence being moved along with the vehicle itself.

Electronic Surveillance

In 1928, the Court heard the case *Olmstead v. United States*. The *Olmstead* case centered on the use of wiretaps by federal agents to listen

to phone calls made and received by Roy Olmstead, a man suspected of bootlegging liquor. *Olmstead* is an especially notable case because it involved the use of wiretaps and was the first Supreme Court ruling involving electronic surveillance of any kind.

Without the use of a search warrant, federal agents placed wiretaps in the basement of Olmstead's building (where he maintained an office) and in areas outside his home. Olmstead was subsequently convicted based on information gathered from the wiretaps. When the case was appealed to the Supreme Court, the Court had to decide whether wiretapping was covered by the protections of the Fourth Amendment.

The Court came to the conclusion that the wiretapping that had occurred in the investigation was not a violation of Olmstead's Fourth Amendment rights. The Court based the ruling upon the fact that the agents had not actually entered into Olmstead's home or office to perform the wiretaps. The Court held that unless it involved an illegal entry into a home or office, the use of wiretapping was not prohibited by the Constitution.

In a dissent to the majority decision, Justice Louis Brandeis argued that the Fourth Amendment was not designed simply to protect

These protesters are demonstrating against domestic wiretapping, which they feel is a violation of the Fourth Amendment. Law enforcement officials believe wiretapping is necessary in order to protect national security.

against the physical invasion of a home, but rather to protect the inherent value of individual privacy. Brandeis wrote, "The progress of science, in furnishing the Government with means of espionage is not likely to stop with wiretapping. Ways may some day be developed by which the Government, without removing papers from secret drawers, can reproduce them in Court, and by which it will be enabled to expose to a jury the most intimate occurrences of the home." Brandeis's overriding concern was the protection of the purpose of the Fourth Amendment, not its literal interpretation.

Katz v. United States

In 1967, the Supreme Court heard *Katz v. United States*. This was a very important Fourth Amendment case because it dealt with electronic

The Federal Communications Act of 1934

In ruling on the *Olmstead* case, Chief Justice William Howard Taft made the claim that the Fourth Amendment protects only physical things, such as papers. Taft believed that the agents in the case had not performed a search nor seized any evidence, but rather they had simply listened to conversations. Based on this logic, Taft ruled that the Fourth Amendment did not apply to wiretapping. He did suggest, however, that Congress could pass laws forbidding wiretaps if they so chose.

Congress did indeed pass a law in 1934 that made it illegal to intercept the private communications of another and to reveal any of the gathered information. The Court subsequently followed the law passed by Congress. In *Nardone v. United States* (1939), the Court's ruling made it clear that federal agents, and indeed anyone else, were forbidden to use wiretapping technology to intercept telephone calls.

surveillance in a public location. Federal agents suspected that Charles Katz was transmitting illegal gambling information using a public phone. An electronic bug was placed on the outside of the phone booth. Because the bug did not in any way penetrate into the interior of the booth, the Court, based on precedent, should have allowed the evidence obtained from the bug.

The Court went against previous rulings, however. It was the opinion of the Court in this case that by closing the door to the booth, Katz had created a space where he could rightfully expect privacy. In the Court's view, it was this expectation of privacy that was the key issue, not the physical placement of the bug on the exterior of the booth.

The Court went further and decided that electronic eavesdropping was a constitutional search, and it fell under the requirements of the Fourth Amendment. A warrant would therefore need to be obtained from a neutral magistrate in order to conduct such a search.

In 1969, the Court continued to lean toward the accused and ruled that any defendants whose rights had been violated by electronic surveillance must have the opportunity to defend themselves against the information gathered. In order to mount a defense, the defendants must be presented with all of the information collected against them. They could then challenge the information that was to be used against them in court.

Drug Testing

Testing for drug use, whether by means of breath, blood, or urine, is another search that has stirred quite a bit of controversy regarding Fourth Amendment rights. The Supreme Court has deemed all such tests as searches and has generally allowed that the tests can be conducted in all cases where public safety is at risk. Thus in 1989, when President Reagan issued an executive order requiring employees of the

U.S. Customs Service to undergo urinalysis drug testing, the Court allowed such a measure to stand.

This type of suspicionless testing is very controversial. Many feel that it is an infringement upon personal freedom. In addition to allowing suspicionless testing for drugs in the workplace, the Court has also held that schools have the right to perform such testing. Such a ruling was passed down in 1995 in *Vernonia School District v. Acton*.

Cutting-Edge Technology

At the time of *Kyllo v. United States*, thermal imaging was a new technology that was not widely available to the general public. It was this criterion that the Court used in disallowing the evidence discovered by the warrantless thermal scans of Danny Kyllo's home. The Court's stance was that if the technology is not in "general public use" then a warrant must be issued before the technology can be used to conduct a search. The Court felt that this standard adequately protected the rights of the individual.

Because of the rapid pace of technological innovation in modern America, maintaining the Fourth Amendment's protections for individuals is certainly not easy. The Court faces a massive

The Transportation Security Administration (TSA) has recently begun to use body scanners in airports around the country. Body scanners have the ability to see through a person's clothes.

task in determining the proper role that new technology can play in future government investigations.

One new technology of note is the body-scanning technology that is being implemented in airports by the Transportation Security

Administration (TSA). Such imaging technology has the ability to see directly through a person's clothes, essentially rendering him or her naked. The TSA asserts that the technology is needed in order to keep airline passengers safe from those who wish to bring weapons or explosives onto flights. Many advocates of individual rights see these searches as pushing, and possibly breaking, the boundaries of our Fourth Amendment rights.

Another very serious technology-based Fourth Amendment issue is the collection and storage of individuals' DNA by government agencies. In 2008, the Newborn Screening Saves Lives Act was passed by the House of Representatives and signed into law by President George W. Bush.

This law allows hospitals to collect and save DNA from every newborn without parental consent. The government's reasoning for the collection is to test newborns for genetic diseases and to prepare the government for various types of public heath emergencies. The collected DNA can then be stored by the government in a central clearinghouse. At this point the DNA becomes the property of the federal government.

The taking of blood, based upon previous Supreme Court rulings, would seem to fall under the category of a search. It is interesting to note, then, that the Newborn Screening Saves Lives Act essentially acts as a general warrant to collect the blood of any newborn at any time and for any purpose to be determined as needed by the government. It is also interesting to note that parental consent is not needed in the collection of the DNA, nor are parents even notified that such a collection is taking place.

Conclusion

When dealing with issues relating to our Fourth Amendment rights, the Supreme Court faces the monumental challenge of balancing the

The USA PATRIOT Act remains a very controversial piece of legislation. Some of the act's provisions have already been struck down by lower courts as unconstitutional.

rights of the individual against the needs of the government to protect national security. Since the terrorist attacks of September 11, 2001, issues of national security have risen to levels of the utmost importance. However difficult the balancing act, the Supreme Court must uphold the Constitution of the United States. This includes ensuring that the individual protections outlined in the Bill of Rights remain real protections that cannot be neglected because of heightened national security.

Two challenges to Fourth Amendment protections have come in the form of the USA PATRIOT Act and Homeland Security Act, which were passed shortly after the September 11, 2001, terrorist attacks. Both of these acts expanded the power of the federal government. Many proponents of individual rights have objected to this expansion of governmental power, as they feel that it impinges upon civil liberties.

Some of the more controversial aspects of the acts are:

- Expanding the government's ability to look at records of an individual's activity being held by third parties. This means, for example, that the government can monitor an individual's Web surfing records as recorded by an Internet service provider.
- Expanding the government's ability to search private property without notice to the owner. Such secret searches represent an obvious threat to established Fourth Amendment protections.
- The expansion of existing exceptions to the Fourth Amendment that had been previously created for collection of foreign intelligence.
- "Trap and trace searches," which expand another Fourth Amendment exception for spying in order to collect information about the origin and destination of certain communications.

Clearly, any expansion of governmental power in America must in turn be checked by the rights of the individual, as outlined in the Bill of Rights. Such is the task that the Supreme Court will face when challenges to the provisions of these new acts eventually find their way to the Court. Indeed, some of the acts' provisions have already been struck down by lower courts as violations of the Fourth Amendment. In 2007, the U.S. District Court of the District of Oregon struck down two provisions of the PATRIOT Act that dealt with searches and intelligence gathering. In giving her ruling, Judge Ann Aiken stated, "It is critical that we, as a democratic nation, pay close attention to traditional Fourth Amendment principles."

AMENDMENTS
TO THE U.S. CONSTITUTION

First Amendment (proposed 1789; ratified 1791): Freedom of religion, speech, press, assembly, and petition

Second Amendment (proposed 1789; ratified 1791): Right to bear arms

Third Amendment (proposed 1789; ratified 1791): No quartering of soldiers in private houses in times of peace

Fourth Amendment (proposed 1789; ratified 1791): Interdiction of unreasonable search and seizure; requirement of search warrants

Fifth Amendment (proposed 1789; ratified 1791): Indictments; due process; self-incrimination; double jeopardy; eminent domain

Sixth Amendment (proposed 1789; ratified 1791): Right to a fair and speedy public trial; notice of accusations; confronting one's accuser; subpoenas; right to counsel

Seventh Amendment (proposed 1789; ratified 1791): Right to a trial by jury in civil cases

Eighth Amendment (proposed 1789; ratified 1791): No excessive bail and fines; no cruel or unusual punishment

Ninth Amendment (proposed 1789; ratified 1791): Protection of unenumerated rights (rights inferred from other legal rights but that are not themselves coded or enumerated in written constitution and laws)

Tenth Amendment (proposed 1789; ratified 1791): Limits the power of the federal government

Eleventh Amendment (proposed 1794; ratified 1795): Sovereign immunity (immunity of states from suits brought by out-of-state citizens and foreigners living outside of states' borders)

Twelfth Amendment (proposed 1803; ratified 1804): Revision of presidential election procedures (electoral college)

Thirteenth Amendment (proposed 1865; ratified 1865): Abolition of slavery

Fourteenth Amendment (proposed 1866; ratified 1868): Citizenship; state due process; application of Bill of Rights to states; revision to apportionment of congressional representatives; denies public office to anyone who has rebelled against the United States

Fifteenth Amendment (proposed 1869; ratified 1870): Suffrage no longer restricted by race

Sixteenth Amendment (proposed 1909; ratified 1913): Allows federal income tax

Seventeenth Amendment (proposed 1912; ratified 1913): Direct election to the U.S. Senate by popular vote

Eighteenth Amendment (proposed 1917; ratified 1919): Prohibition of alcohol

Nineteenth Amendment (proposed 1919; ratified 1920): Women's suffrage

Twentieth Amendment (proposed 1932; ratified 1933): Term commencement for Congress (January 3) and president (January 20)

Twenty-first Amendment (proposed 1933; ratified 1933): Repeal of Eighteenth Amendment (Prohibition)

Twenty-second Amendment (proposed 1947; ratified 1951): Limits president to two terms

Twenty-third Amendment (proposed 1960; ratified 1961): Representation of District of Columbia in electoral college

Twenty-fourth Amendment (proposed 1962; ratified 1964): Prohibition of restriction of voting rights due to nonpayment of poll taxes

Twenty-fifth Amendment (proposed 1965; ratified 1967): Presidential succession

Twenty-sixth Amendment (proposed 1971; ratified 1971): Voting age of eighteen

Twenty-seventh Amendment (proposed 1789; ratified 1992): Congressional compensation

Proposed but Unratified Amendments

Congressional Apportionment Amendment (proposed 1789; still technically pending): Apportionment of U.S. representatives

Titles of Nobility Amendment (proposed 1810; still technically pending): Prohibition of titles of nobility

Corwin Amendment (proposed 1861; still technically pending though superseded by Thirteenth Amendment): Preservation of slavery

Child Labor Amendment (proposed 1924; still technically pending): Congressional power to regulate child labor

Equal Rights Amendment (proposed 1972; expired): Prohibition of inequality of men and women

District of Columbia Voting Rights Amendment (proposed 1978; expired): District of Columbia voting rights

GLOSSARY

admissible evidence Proof or testimony that is allowed to be presented during proceedings in a court of law.

controversy A dispute or argument between sides holding opposing views.

conviction The act or process of finding or proving someone guilty.

defendant A person who has been accused of committing a crime.

delegate A person chosen to speak, act, or otherwise represent others.

effects A person's personal belongings.

evasion Escaping or avoiding something.

evidence Facts or signs that help one to find out the truth or come to a conclusion.

exclusion To leave something out.

magistrate A local law official, such as the judge of a police court.

obtain To gain or get by means of planning or effort.

overrule To reject or decide against.

parliament A legislature of a nation such as Canada or Great Britain.

possession The condition of having or owning something.

precedent A model or example that may be followed or referred to later.

probable cause A reliable reason to believe that something may be true; in law, the grounds for suspicion for making a search.

prosecute To begin and carry on legal action against a person who has been accused of an offense.

ratify To make something legal by official approval.

rebellion Open, organized opposition toward an organization or entity, such as a government.

search warrant An official document that authorizes a search.

suspect Someone who is thought to have committed a crime.

FOR MORE INFORMATION

Colonial Williamsburg
P.O. Box 1776
Williamsburg, VA 23187-1776
(757) 229-1000
Web site: http://www.history.org
A visit to Colonial Williamsburg, the world's largest "living" history museum, lets visitors take a step back in time to witness life in colonial America. Many of the exhibits are housed in original or restored eighteenth-century buildings and homes.

Fraunces Tavern Museum
54 Pearl Street
New York, NY 10004-2429
(212) 425-1778
Web site: http://www.fraucestavernmuseum.org
Operated by the Sons of the Revolution, the Fraunces Tavern Museum opened its doors in 1907. It houses eight galleries of displays that document various aspects of life in colonial America and the early republic.

James Madison Museum
129 Caroline Street
Orange, VA 22960-1532
(540) 672-1776
Web site: http://www.jamesmadisonmus.org
The James Madison Museum is home to various exhibits about the father of the Bill of the Rights, James Madison, and life in rural Virginia.

The National Archives Experience

Constitution Avenue NW

Between 7th Street and 9th Street

Washington, DC 20408

(877) 444-6777

Web site: http://www.archives.gov/nae/visit

The public vaults at the archives let visitors interact with American history. Guests can access more than one thousand records, from presidential audio recordings and historic maps and photographs to facsimiles of important documents. The Rotunda for the Charters of Freedom houses the Declaration of Independence, the Constitution, and the Bill of Rights.

National Constitution Center

Independence Mall

525 Arch Street

Philadelphia, PA 19106

(866) 917-1787

Web site: http://constitutioncenter.org

The National Constitution Center in Philadelphia is an interactive history museum. The museum is devoted to the U.S. Constitution and promoting the story of American democracy.

National Museum of American History

National Mall

14th Street and Constitution Avenue NW

Washington, DC 20560

(202) 633-1000

Web site: http://americanhistory.si.edu

For people of all ages, a visit to the National Museum of American History can be an event that provides a deep and fundamental understanding of what it means to be an American.

National Museum of Crime & Punishment
575 7th Street NW
Washington, DC 20004
(202) 621-5550
Web site: http://www.crimemuseum.org
This massive museum includes over one hundred interactive exhibits and artifacts pertaining to America's history of crime prevention and law enforcement.

Web Sites

Due to the changing nature of Internet links, Rosen Publishing has developed an online list of Web sites related to the subject of this book. This site is updated regularly. Please use this link to access the list:

http://www.rosenlinks.com/ausc/4th

FOR FURTHER READING

Bridegam, Martha. *Search and Seizure*. Philadelphia, PA: Chelsea House Publishers, 2005.

Head, Tom, ed. *The Bill of Rights* (Interpreting Primary Documents). San Diego, CA: Greenhaven Press, 2004.

Kuhn, Betsy. *Prying Eyes: Privacy in the Twenty-First Century*. Minneapolis, MN: Twenty-First Century Books, 2008.

Labunski, Richard. *James Madison and the Struggle for the Bill of Rights*. New York, NY: Oxford University Press, 2006.

Leavitt, Amie Jane. *The Declaration of Independence in Translation: What It Really Means*. Mankato, MN: Capstone Press, 2009.

McInnis, Thomas N. *The Evolution of the Fourth Amendment*. Lanham, MD: Lexington Books, 2009.

Monk, Linda R. *The Bill of Rights: A User's Guide*. 4th ed. Alexandria, VA: Close Up Publishing, 2004.

Roberts, Jeremy. *James Madison*. Minneapolis, MN: Lerner Publishing Group, 2004.

Smith, Rich. *Fourth Amendment: The Right to Privacy*. Edina, MN: ABDO Publishing Company, 2008.

Taylor-Butler, Christine. *The Bill of Rights*. New York, NY: Children's Press, 2008.

Tubb, Kristin O'Donnell. *Freedom from Unfair Searches and Seizures* (Bill of Rights). Farmington Hills, MI: Greenhaven Press, 2005.

BIBLIOGRAPHY

American Civil Liberties Union. "Surveillance Under the USA/PATRIOT Act." Retrieved April 1, 2010 (http://www.aclu.org/technology-and-liberty/surveillance-under-usapatriot-act).

Bodenhamer, David J., and James W. Ely Jr., eds. *The Bill of Rights in Modern America*. Bloomington, IN: Indiana University Press, 2008.

The Constitution of the United States, Bill of Rights.

Cornell University Law School. "Kyllo v. The United States." Retrieved April 1, 2010 (http://www.law.cornell.edu/supct/html/99-8508.ZS.html).

Dudley, William, ed. *The Bill of Rights: Opposing Viewpoints*. San Diego, CA: Greenhaven Press, 1994.

Fourth Amendment Summaries. "Fourth Amendment Case Decisions of the United States Supreme Court." Retrieved April 1, 2010 (http://www.fourthamendmentsummaries.com).

Head, Tom, ed. *The Bill of Rights* (Interpreting Primary Documents). San Diego, CA: Greenhaven Press, 2004.

Konvitz, Milton R. *Fundamental Rights: History of a Constitutional Doctrine*. New Brunswick, NJ: Transaction Publishers, 2001.

Kukla, Jon, ed. *The Bill of Rights: A Lively Heritage*. Richmond, VA: Virginia State Library and Archives, 1987.

Labunski, Richard. *James Madison and the Struggle for the Bill of Rights*. New York, NY: Oxford University Press, 2006.

McInnis, Thomas N. *The Evolution of the Fourth Amendment*. Lanham, MD: Lexington Books, 2009.

Meserve, Jeanne, and Mike M. Ahlers. "Full Body Scanners Improve Security, TSA Says." Retrieved April 1, 2010 (http://www.cnn.com/2010/TRAVEL/04/01/airport.body.scanners/index.html).

National Archives. "The Charters of Freedom: A New World Is at Hand." Retrieved April 1, 2010 (http://www.archives.gov/exhibits/charters/bill_of_rights.html).

New American. "TSA and the Fourth Amendment: Take Another Look." Retrieved April 1, 2010 (http://www.thenewamerican.com/index.php/usnews/constitution/3091-tsa-and-the-fourth-amendment-take-another-look).

Ramasastry, Anita. "Reform the Patriot Act to Ensure Civil Liberties." CNN.com. Retrieved April 1, 2010 (http://www.cnn.com/2005/LAW/04/20/ramasastry.patriotact/index.html).

Ramen, Fred. *The Right to Freedom from Searches*. New York, NY: Rosen Publishing, 2001.

Smith, Christopher E. *Constitutional Rights: Myths and Realities*. Belmont, CA: Wadsworth, 2004.

Smith, Rich. *Fourth Amendment: The Right to Privacy*. Edina, MN: ABDO Publishing Company, 2008.

Street Law, Inc., and the Supreme Court Historical Society. "Landmark Supreme Court Cases." Retrieved April 1, 2010 (http://www.landmarkcases.org).

Tribe, Laurence H. "Bush Stomps on the Fourth Amendment." Retrieved April 1, 2010 (http://www.boston.com/news/globe/editorial_opinion/oped/articles/2006/05/16/bush_stomps_on_fourth_amendment).

INDEX

About the Author

Dean Galiano is a writer who lives and works in New York City. He has written a number of books about American history, including *Crossing the Delaware: George Washington and the Battle of Trenton* and the six-book series Famous American Trails.

Photo Credits

Cover (left) Alex Wong/Getty Images; cover (middle) Mark Ralston/ AFP/Getty Images; cover (right) Robert Nickelsberg/Getty Images; p. 1 (top) © www.istockphoto.com/Tom Nulens; p. 1 (bottom) © www. istockphoto.com/Lee Pettet; p. 3 © www.istockphoto.com/Nic Taylor; pp. 4–5, 28–29, 32, 49 © AP Images; pp. 8, 18, 25, 40 © www.istockphoto. com/arturbo; pp. 9, 13, 15 Library of Congress Prints and Photographs Division; p. 10 Fotosearch/Getty Images; p. 16 MPI/Getty Images; p. 20 © Philip Mould, Ltd., London/Bridgeman Art Library; pp. 22, 38–39 Stockbyte/Thinkstock; p. 31 Hulton Archive/Getty Images; p. 34 Gene Forte/Consolidated News Pictures/Getty Images; p. 36 Cynthia Johnson/Time & Life Pictures/Getty Images; p. 41 David McNew/ Getty Images; pp. 42–43 Tim Boyle/Getty Images; pp. 46–47 Chip Somodevilla/Getty Images.

Editor: Karolena Bielecki; Photo Researcher: Amy Feinberg